BLISSFUL LIVING
journal

ASHLINA KAPOSTA

Copyright 2018 Ashlina Kaposta
ISTA Publications

All rights reserved. This book may not be reproduced in whole or in part, stored in a retrieval system, or transmitted in any form or by any means — electronic, mechanical, or other — without written permission from the publisher, except by a reviewer, who may quote brief passages in a review.

DISCLAIMER: This publication contains the opinions and ideas of its author. The advice contained herein is for informational purposes only. Please consult a medical professional before beginning any diet or exercise program. The author disclaims all responsibility for any liability, loss, risk, injury, or damage resulting from the use, proper or improper, of any of the contents contained in this book. Every effort has been made to ensure that the information contained in this book is complete and accurate.

ISBN: 978-1718719873
Printed in the United States of America

Dedication

This book is dedicated to my baby boy Roman. Thank you for choosing me to be your mommy. You coming into my life has shown me who I really am. I will love you forever and beyond.

Acknowledgements

A big thank you to my beautiful soul sisters, my readers who encourage and inspire me to write everyday. I love being on this journey with you.

A wild moment of gratitude for my illustrator **Wenna Prive.**

TABLE OF CONTENTS

INTRODUCTION:
GETTING BACK TO BLISS
THE POWER OF JOURNALING
30 DAYS OF JOURNALING

BLISSFULNESS:
BLISS BOOSTERS
DAILY
WEEKLY
MONTHLY

MINDFULNESS:
CULTIVATING MINDFULNESS
8 ATTITUDES OF MINDFULNESS
REFLECTION JOURNALING

SOULFULNESS:
CONNECTING TO YOUR SOUL
EMOTIONAL HEALING
LIMITING BELIEFS JOURNALING

FORGIVENESS:
LETTING IT ALL GO
JOURNALING

ILLUMINATION:
POWERFUL MANIFESTATION
8 STEPS TO MANIFESTING
BECOME WHO YOU WERE MEANT TO BE JOURNALING
DIVINE FEMININE

"I withdraw from people and places from time to time. **I need space** from a world that is filled with millions of mouths that talk too much but never have anything to say"

-Kaitlin Foster

INTRODUCTION

"We are all like a clay Buddha, covered with a shell of hardness created out of fear, and yet underneath each of us is a 'golden Buddha'." - Jack Canfield

If you are anything like me you have spent some time reading your share of inspirational books. Reading books is one of my absolute favorite forms of self care, it is something I will just never get enough of. One of those books I grew to love is Chicken Soup for the Soul and one story in particular always stuck with me. It's the story Jack Canfield shares about his trip to Thailand and his experience with The Temple of the Golden Buddha.

The Siamese monks, realizing they were about to be attacked, covered their precious golden Buddha with a layer of clay to hide it from the Burmese. Sadly, all of the Siamese monks were killed leaving a huge clay buddha head. Hundreds of years later, in 1957, a group of monks were relocating the clay Buddha and one of them discovered a peek of golden light shining through the clay. Curiously, he began to chisel away at the clay to see what was underneath. After breaking off several shards of clay, he discovered what was underneath was a large, brightly beaming golden Buddha.

In Jack Canfield's story, he shares with us, *"We are all like a clay Buddha, covered with a shell of hardness created out of fear, and yet underneath each of us is a 'golden Buddha', a 'golden Christ' or a 'golden essence', which is our real self. Somewhere along the way between the ages of two and nine, we begin to cover up our golden essence, our natural self. Much like the monk with the hammer and the chisel, our task now is to discover our true essence once again."*

The first time I read this story, it gave me chills. It was one of those moments where I had a personal epiphany. We spend years and years building layers of clay around our true inner essence, hiding our light from shining in the world because of fears we develop over the course of our lives. In order to live a life of true bliss, we must chisel away at the layers of clay, letting ourselves become who we really are at the core. That's who God intended us to be anyway.

From that moment on I decided to take on the challenge of chiseling away at my own layers of clay covering my golden essence, in an effort to move past fears, live a fulfilling life and let my light shine brightly.

BACK TO BLISS

Did you know that everything you have ever wanted is actually meant for you? It's quite possible you just haven't had the courage to believe that you are worthy and deserving of the things that your heart truly desires. We are programmed and conditioned by society to believe that the grass is always greener on the other side and what we have is never enough, therefore we can never be truly living and thriving in a way that makes us feel blissful. It seems to me we are a society that is always chasing after someone else's dream. The real question we've got to ask ourselves is, *"do I even know what it is that I really want?"*

Over the years I have learned that in order to design the life that I dream of, I have to know deep within my heart what it is that I truly desire and why I desire it. I've had to learn the art of cultivating my intuition, dropping all my limiting beliefs and subconscious fear based thinking patterns. For years, I allowed what I was "supposed to be doing" or "what was working for someone else" guide my path when it wasn't clear for me to see for myself. Most of us unintentionally live this way, being available for a life of satisfaction, as they say "if it ain't broke, don't fix it". We live day in day out, comfortable and fully complacent with our lives, even thought deep down, we know we aren't satisfied or blissfully happy.

However, on my journey of pursuing self-growth, cultivating my spirituality and personal development, I have learned that if we aren't living our lives deeply fulfilled, totally thriving, lit up with purpose and passion, we are missing out on the life we are meant to be living. We aren't stepping into the greatness that God is calling us to walk into. This is what causes us to feel deep inside that something is missing or this is when we get blocked from being able to manifest the things we want in our lives.

You see, we are meant to have everything we want, be expansive, wealthy, thriving, blissfully living out our days on this Earth. It's supposed to be easy, we are the ones who have made it complicated for ourselves simply by believing that its meant to be hard or feeling we are undeserving. Blissful living is what God and the universe is craving from us. At our core, our true self holds the key to all the things in the world that we desire. It is my soul intent to share with you what I know about how to unlock and unleash your golden essence so that you may call in, all that is meant for you in this life.

I've created this journal to show you how to go within, get connected to your true essence, begin to trust yourself, walk into your divine purpose and live out your bliss!

THE POWER OF JOURNALING

Taking the time to connect to yourself gives you back your life. Even though you may feel you have wasted so much time, the truth is, you are right on time! Time is just an illusion. Once you take the time out for yourself to go within, you will gain the clarity and confidence you need to navigate your life with power.

Over the course of the thirty days that you go through this journal, I encourage you to schedule in time for the bliss boosters on page 50. These will serve as your support for keeping your vibe and energy high during your work in this journal.

Spending even five minutes each day connecting to yourself will create big shifts for you. It will help you uncover your golden essence, heal past pain and discover your true inner self. It's a great adventure. The best part is, it's free and you can start today! Placing a connection with yourself and your intuition as a priority every single day will show the universe your ready for your dreams and your blissful life will soon begin.

I have created this journal in sections to use as a guide to bring you back to your original essence of bliss that you came into this world with. Use this journal to help you uncover who you really are at the core. Allow the experience to be blissful, beautiful and glamorous...

xo Ashlina

DAY ONE

Who are YOU? Describe yourself in detail. What do you believe in? What do you love in your life? What are your favorite things about yourself?

I care about others, I'm trying to better myself, I'm smart, I can learn things quickly. I want my daughter to grow up with confidence that she is beautiful & deserves the best in life & should never settle. I want my son to be happy & confident, respectful to women, to thrive. I want to be surrounded with family when I'm older. To have enough $ that I am set for the rest of my life & can give some to my children. I want my husband to be happy, to allow him to explore his passions as he has allowed me to explore mine. I want to feel wanted & loved, I want to feel like I matter. I love my sister, I have an amazingly supportive, patient, kind, loving sister. I believe everyone deserves love & should be treated fairly. I love that we have bought & sold almost 4 houses now.

DAY TWO

Who is the woman you aspire to be? Use the space on these two pages to create a visual representation of the best version of yourself. Your style, your habits, values, hobbies, home, relationships, etc. Dream up your most beautiful YOU!

Working on myself daily

reading

♡ More romance with my husband

outside more ☀

Raising Respectful Children
happy, confident, adventurous

garage parties

combined making $400K a year

Traveling - Japan, Paris, Egypt, Greece

full time caregiver for Cavan

stylish outfits

beautifully designed home

group of good friends

Constantly Creating

Laughter happiness

Yoga Retreat
Yoga

Fit bodies - healthy
Work out everyday

business owner (Children's Boutique)

self employed (electrology)
my own studio @ home

Loved as I am
feel wanted

Confidence

always learning

DAY THREE

What part of yourself have you been holding back in order to make other people comfortable?

ADVENTURE!
- Moving somewhere else so my family isn't upset

- Trying new things for risk of failure/dissapointment.

- Trying to just make $ to make others happy/satisfied with me.

- Not sharing my goals, new interests in fear of rejection or hearing their fears which in turn makes me question & fearful

DAY FOUR

Is there something in your life you need to let go of but have a hard time doing so?

Approval from dad

DAY FIVE

Are you good at receiving? Compliments? Gifts? Affection? Attention? Why or why not?

DAY SIX

What are your top ten priorities? How do you spend your time?

1._____

2._____

3._____

4._____

5._____

6._____

7._____

8._____

9._____

10._____

DAY SEVEN

Are you good at keeping commitments and sticking to your word? If not, why?

DAY EIGHT

What are you wanting to experience more of in your life? List anything like Love, activities, friendships, family time, financial freedom, etc.

DAY NINE

Is there anything you have been lying to yourself about? How can you tell yourself the truth?

DAY TEN

Do you feel that your life is aligned with your true purpose? If not, what can you do to rearrange things so that it is?

DAY ELEVEN

How are your relationships going in your life? With whom are you feeling resistance?

Ho'oponopono...

is the Hawaiian practice of reconciliation and forgiveness. When you feel like something isn't right between you and another person, it can cause illness to the soul and block your bliss.

While it can be hard to make amends, you can use the Ho'oponopono prayer to help forgive others, the situation and yourself in order to heal your inner self. The prayer is simple. All you have to do is closer your eyes and visualize the person or situation that you feel needs amends. Then say the following prayer while you imagine releasing all energetic ties to that situation.

I AM SORRY

PLEASE FORGIVE ME

I LOVE YOU

THANK YOU

There have been a few times where I found myself creatively blocked. My mentors would encourage me to make sure I didn't need to make amends or forgive anyone. Many times I found that it wasn't about anyone else, I really needed to forgive myself. This prayer has worked for me every time. It's important that we let go and forgive any situation that causes us to feel bad about ourselves or life so that we can stay in a positive and vibrant energy state. Especially when it comes to ourselves, this is one of the ultimate acts of self love.

DAY TWELVE
Do you know your values in life? List 10 important life values below:

_____
_____
_____
_____
_____
_____
_____
_____
_____
_____
_____

Are you truly living in integrity? *Meaning your values line up with your actions in life.*

_____
_____
_____
_____
_____
_____
_____
_____
_____
_____
_____

DAY THIRTEEN

Are you making time to connect with your inner child? *You do this by channeling your creative side through things like painting, dancing, singing, laughing, being adventurous, etc.*

DAY FOURTEEN

What are some repeating issues you seem to come up against again and again in life. *This could be finances, relationships, career aspects, etc.*

DAY FIFTEEN

What are some of your fear based beliefs? *Things like "I'm too old", "I am not good enough", "I'll never have enough"*

DAY SIXTEEN

Is there anything you can think of that your inner self may want to heal? Any repressed emotions you've been holding inside? Let them out fully now.

DAY SEVENTEEN
Describe what success means and looks like to you.

DAY EIGHTEEN

What is tugging at your heart that you would like to accomplish this year?

DAY NINETEEN

If you received $50,000 today, how would you spend it? List out exactly what you would spend it on and make sure you account for every penny!

DAY TWENTY
If money weren't an issue, what would you be doing differently in your day to day life?

DAY TWENTY ONE

What hobbies and commitments in your life aren't good for you? Why? Describe how you can walk away from what isn't serving your highest self.

DAY TWENTY TWO

Are you experiencing any issues with jealousy or competition? With whom and why?

_____
_____
_____
_____
_____
_____
_____
_____
_____
_____
_____

How can you view others in a more positive way?

_____
_____
_____
_____
_____
_____
_____
_____
_____
_____
_____

DAY TWENTY THREE

What are you the most grateful for in your life and why?

DAY TWENTY FOUR

How are you handling time management? Are you frantic and stressed or lazy and unmotivated? Explain.

DAY TWENTY FIVE

Have I experienced serendipity? List a few of your favorite moments of serendipity, when you truly felt supported by God/the Universe.

DAY TWENTY SIX

What are your favorite ways to get yourself into a higher vibration? List your top 12 favorites.

1. _____

2. _____

3. _____

4. _____

5. _____

6. _____

7. _____

8. _____

9. _____

10. _____

11. _____

12. _____

DAY TWENTY SEVEN

What is one thing you would like to work on improving in your life? Describe what it would feel like for you to have that happen in your life tomorrow.

DAY TWENTY EIGHT

Is there anything inside of you that is dying to be born? This could be a book, a dream, a song, a creative project? What is your inner self needing to express?

DAY TWENTY NINE
Are you living your life from the heart or from the mind? Describe your relationship with your intuition.

DAY THIRTY
What would a blissful day look like to you?

"If you do **follow your bliss**, you put yourself on a kind of track that has been there all the while, waiting for you and the life you ought to be living"

-Joseph Campbell

BLISSFULNESS

BLISS BOOSTERS

Bliss Boosters are your daily, weekly, and monthly tools that will enhance your everyday life experiences. When you intentionally implement these into your life, you will become more aligned with your joy, confidence, intuition and your deepest aspirations. They will help you amp up your energy and get in the frequency of your dreams. Each of these is powerful when you do them with your heart, so make sure you have fun while doing them.

The key is to continually be raising your energy and vibration to your bliss zone so that you naturally magnetize your desires to you. When you are aligned with bliss in your life, you become a powerful creator. You can't manifest the things you dream of, unless you are an energetic match to them. Staying in a high vibration is essential for manifesting and designing a life of bliss.

Self development is difficult work. There will be times that fear and doubt can't help but creep into your thinking. However, if you keep yourself active with your personal bliss boosters, these feel good activities will help you to stay at a high vibration and energy.

Take a look at your calendar over the next month and schedule these in before anything else so you won't drop the ball and forget to do them. Your goal is to stay following your bliss. If there are days you don't feel like journaling or digging into these questions, implement one of the bliss boosters into your day first, then get back to work. The work you do will be amplified by your connection to your blissful intuition and spirituality, which makes it more likely to really stick.

Allow your home to serve as your sanctuary and spend time creating the space to do this beautiful soul work. Light candles, play mood music, get in your most comfortable chair. I like to sage my space first and have gorgeous crystals all around me when I do any rituals at home. Get yourself into the process, imagine that you are already living in your dream home and don't take things too seriously. If it isn't perfect now, its okay, it will be soon and I promise it will be so much fun.

DAILY

1. Morning Routines: You want to begin your day on a positive note. Welcome each day with intentional actions like yoga stretches, fresh water with lemon, affirmations, lighting a beautiful candle. Make it your own special routine.

2. Meditation & Movement: Whether you set your Apple Watch to breathe for one minute, go for a brisk walk or you follow along with a 5 minute guided meditation, take some time to get silent and go within. I recommend chakra balancing guided meditations on YouTube, they are fun and really healing.

3. Dress up for your dreams: Make sure that everyday you let your style shine. Dress up as the woman you desire to be. Show off your personality in what you wear out in the world and also while at home. Accessorize with flair.

4. Practice Journaling: Each day spend time writing down your inner most thoughts on feelings. This is a great way to brain dump, and at the same time it helps you connect to your intuition.

5. Eat your fruits and vegetables: Make sure to get adequate amounts of water and nutrients. Eat in such a way that has you focused on nourishing your body. Experiment, try a veggie burger or making a smoothie.

6. Commit to your skin and body care: Take your vitamins daily. I suggest sticking with a multi-vitamin, Biotin and B-12. Also, make sure you have a good skin care regimen that keeps you glowing and fresh.

7. Practice gratitude: This is a must! Each day I write one thing I am thankful for in my planner. You can also practice saying a gratitude statement when you sit down to eat or do small things like light your favorite candle.

8. Check in with your emotions: Always be sure to listen to your feelings. Don't fight negative feelings, use them as guide posts for when you need more self love. Staying in a high vibration is essential for manifesting and designing a life of bliss.

9. Nightly Routine: End your day with kisses and hugs to your loved ones and pets. Turn off electronics. Take a long hot bath. Read a book. Drink a cup of mint tea. Wind down in a positive way that feels good to you.

NOTES on DAILY BLISS BOOSTERS
How and when will you incorporate your favorites?

WEEKLY

1. Bring home fresh flowers: You want to surround yourself with life energy and fresh flowers are a great way to boost your own bliss.

2. Get into a creative flow: Take a break from technology and get into your creative flow. Look at magazines, color, paint, create a page in an art journal, etc. Tap into your creative energy and detox from the digital world.

3. Blissful Baths: This sacred ritual is such a therapeutic and healing practice. Light candles, add bath salts, play music, drink tea. Make it a special thing for yourself to clear your mind and heal your soul.

4. Drink a cleansing green juice: I always enjoy grabbing a kombucha tea or beautiful green juice when I am at the grocery store. I don't get around to it everyday but if you can aim to do this at least once a week, you will be better for doing it. For me, I like to play around with Wellness Wednesday and make an effort to drink my juices on that day.

5. Clutter Clear: Give yourself a day of the week where you sort through your mail, clear off your entryway table, go through bills, etc. You will feel lighter after doing so.

6. Go on a creative adventure: Take a little excursion for at least an hour or two where you head somewhere that inspires you. Go to a local art gallery, hit up your library or visit a boutique that inspires you.

7. Write a love note: Reach out to a friend, family member or mentor and write them a note of love and appreciation. Getting letters in the mail is such a good feeling. Why not send that love out into the world.

8. Take a yoga class: Yoga is such a beautiful way to get in deep breathing, mindfulness and body stretching. You will feel fantastic after the class, you may even have a breakthrough.

9. Have an inspiring conversation: Many of my friends live in different states, so we have dates where we catch up over the phone. There is nothing quite as healing as chatting with an inspiring friend who loves and supports you. Keep yourself in the company and conversation of positive and happy people.

NOTES on WEEKLY BLISS BOOSTERS
How and when will you incorporate your favorites?

MONTHLY

1. Journal your monthly dreams and goals: At the start of each month, make a list of the things that you want to experience during the month.

2. Go shopping for crystals: Celebrate your accomplishments with gifts for you and your home! I love shopping for new, beautiful crystals to use during meditations and display in my home.

3. Get a mani/pedi: You will always feel better when your nails and feet look beautiful and polished. It's absolutely part of an outfit. It's essential to always be feeling your absolute best!

4. Host a soiree: Have some friends over for dinner or wine, have a game night, host a vision board party or even a Sunday brunch. Making memories through entertaining will keep your life full.

5. Study something new: You can always light up your life by implementing new hobbies into your schedule and adding value to your talent list. Try your hand at gardening, a writing class, learn how to speak French or even practice photography!

6. Read a book or two: One of the best practices to do before you drift off to sleep is reading. It helps to get your brain into the deep slumber mood. Choose something uplifting or exciting.

7. Make body appointments: I swear by my chiropractor. I also love massages, Reiki healings, acupuncturists and massages. Your body is a temple. Take excellent care of it.

8. Decorate a beautiful vignette: Decor is the ultimate way to enhance your bliss. I love create beautiful stylings in my home. You can set a gorgeous dinner table scape, re-arrange your fireplace mantle or set up a spiritual altar. Make new arrangements with your current favorite things.

9. Give Back: Every once in a while its nice to get out of your world and do something for someone else. Pick one thing a month you can do to help heal the planet, feed the homeless, give time to animals or help a friend get organized.

10. Do a home cleansing ritual. Whether you use, sage, Palo Santo, windex or incense clear out the energy in your home. This is your sanctuary and it needs to have a good energetic flow to support you in living your best life.

NOTES on MONTHLY BLISS BOOSTERS
How and when will you incorporate your favorites?

Focus inside on **bliss**. Think thoughts of **bliss**. Feel **blissful**. See yourself in **bliss**. As you connect to the **bliss** inside you more often, your whole world will shift to reflect that **bliss**. The Universe will move people, circumstances and events to deliver **bliss** to you - because you are magnetizing **bliss**.

MINDFULNESS

CULTIVATING MINDFULNESS

As we begin to create a life filled with bliss and all of our wildest dreams, we have to open ourselves to shift how we currently approach life. We are going to touch on each area of life and how we can improve them but its important that we first begin with the mind. Our minds dictate our attitude and overall life experience. Practicing mindfulness is key to making these blissful shifts with ease.

In the book, *A Mindfulness-Based Stress Reduction Workbook*, by Elisha and Bob Stahl, mindfulness is described as "being fully aware of whatever is happening in the present moment, without filters or the lens of judgment. It can be brought to any situation. Put simply, mindfulness consists of cultivating awareness of the mind and body and living in the here and now." The book goes on to explain the eight attitudes of mindfulness that would be wise for us to adopt and put into practice.

THE 8 ATTITUDES OF MINDFULNESS

Beginner's mind. This quality is the ability to see things as if for the very first time, with a sense of curiosity and openness. It's a child like wonder. You look at things with a perspective of endless possibilities.

Non-judgment. This quality of awareness involves not labeling thoughts, feelings, or sensations as good or bad, right or wrong, fair or unfair, but simply taking note of thoughts, feelings, or sensations in each moment.

Acknowledgment. This quality of awareness validates and acknowledges things as they are.

Non-striving. With this awareness you move with the flow of life. There is no grasping, aversion to change, or movement away from whatever arises in the moment; in other words, non-striving means not trying to get anywhere other than where you are.

Equanimity. This involves having balance and fostering wisdom. It allows for a deep understanding of the nature of change and allows you to be with change with greater insight and compassion.

Letting be. With this quality of awareness, you can simply let things be as they are, with no need to try to let go of whatever is present.

Self-reliance. This quality of awareness helps you see for yourself, from your own experience, what is true or untrue.

Self-compassion. This quality of awareness cultivates love for yourself as you are, without self-blame, or criticism.

What 'attitudes of mindfulness' do I need to be more focused on?

In what areas of my life would I benefit from mindfulness the most?

Parenting

Business

Relationships

Internal Happiness

List a few situations in your life that are in need of a more mindful attitude. How can you see things differently?

One day she discovered
that she was fierce,
and strong,
and full of fire.
Not even she could
hold herself back
because her
passion burned
brighter than her fears.

-Mark Anthony

SOULFULNESS

CONNECTING TO YOUR SOUL

Before I was ever able to get to know my true inner self, I was a person who was constantly looking outside myself for everything. When it came to every area of my life, I made decisions based on what everyone else seemed to be doing. If there was a class, I took it, a book, I read it. I was just *that* girl. After years of self help workshops, vision board creating, watching The Secret countless times, I finally had a huge moment of breakthrough after a deeply spiritual conversation with my life coach. **I am responsible for what I am experiencing in my life. I alone hold the power to create the life I want to live.**

I know it sounds a little cliche' but up until that point I truly believed that God was responsible for everything that happened in our lives. It never occurred to me that I was actually a co-creator of my reality. It took a while for it to sink in but once it actually did, I was never again the same.

I began to ask myself the very questions from this journal to uncover my true inner self. I began to acknowledge that as a direct result of my own fears, judgements, feelings and subconscious beliefs, I was creating a reality in my life that reflected back to me those very feelings, thoughts and beliefs. They played out in all my life experiences. It was then I knew that taking charge of my life would involve taking full responsibility for everything I was experiencing as my own personal choice.

Now knowing that every word, thought, action and feeling carries an energetic vibration that radiates out into the universe, I began to see how I could start shifting the outcomes. These vibrations have an immediate effect on our overall sense of well-being. If I would just pay attention to my mental, emotional and physical body, I could tune into these parts of myself to give me clues as to what sort of experiences I would currently be attracting. I knew that in order to manifest nothing but joyful experiences, like pure love, abundance, wealth, vibrancy, freedom, I would have to be experiencing bliss in all parts of my self. Mind, body and soul.

It was then that I made the decision to live from a #blissvibesonly perspective. If I was feeling less than blissful in any part of myself, I would immediately create a new opportunity to remedy that. In a sense, I began to work on healing myself, one thought, emotion and feeling at a time.

EMOTIONAL HEALING

    Once I knew that I had some serious work to do, I was terrified because deep down, I didn't really trust myself. I had a hard time knowing if a feeling or emotion was real or not. I had to be willing and ready to go deep within, really allowing all of me to come to the surface. Repressed emotions from childhood, desires I never wanted to believe that I had, etc.

    In order to become the most vibrant, confident, free and fullest version of yourself, you have to be comfortable getting intimate with your inner most self and begin to trust EVERYTHING that comes from within. No judgements.

    I was introduced to a 6 step emotional healing process from one of my girlfriends and I think it would be helpful for you to use if you find yourself in need of your own healing. Feel free to use this system however you would like, it is simply here as a guide post for you to do your own inner work.

THE 6 STEPS TO EMOTIONAL HEALING

Recognize the trigger & Acknowledge the emotion. Allow yourself to fully feel every emotion that pops into your day. Anger, jealousy, fear, hurt, frustration, sadness, etc. Give yourself permission to experience the depth so that you don't deny the spontaneous release of that emotion.

Don't judge yourself or the emotion. Simply acknowledge its existence and observe. Look for where the uncomfortable root emotion is and where it stems from. The emotions are just reflections from the past, a messenger from your inner self that says "I need healing".

Nurturing your inner self. Give yourself some space where you can quiet yourself and check in. Act as if you are mothering your own emotions. Ask yourself… why am I feeling this way? When was the last time I felt this way? Show yourself compassion and acknowledge your feelings as valid. Say to yourself "I am completely here with and for you right now".

Forgiveness. Think of your inner self as a wounded little child who is just looking for some loving. Forgive yourself for anything that comes up for you. Doing so releases your body from any restriction.

Change limiting beliefs. Talk yourself out of any negative stories or beliefs about yourself. Change them to viewing all situations as positive for you. Show yourself why you deserve all the love in the world.

Acceptance. Begin to accept that you can't change situations or people. The only thing you can do is to change how you think or feel about yourself. Keep on loving yourself and being your own best friend.

List the emotional triggers that cause you to react in a way that does not feel good to you:

1. yelling
2. Being overwhelmed in my head with ideas/goals
3. Cavan crying/upset
4. Thoughts about mistakes I've made
5. Dad being upset w/ me or angry
6. Things that happened to me in the past
7.
8.
9.
10.
11.
12.

Questions you can use to prompt diving deep through triggers & difficult experiences:

How does this make me feel and why?

___

When was the last time I have experienced this emotion?

___

When did I first experience this feeling in my life?

___

What is the possible serendipity of this challenge?

What have I learned about myself here?

When you're in a dark place, you sometimes **tend to think** you've been buried.

Perhaps you've been **planted**.

Bloom.

LIMITING BELIEFS

List your top 10 beliefs that block or limit you. Perhaps something your mother or father said to you when you were little. It could also be things like, what society tells you to believe. For example "You are too old, too short, not educated enough, not lucky enough, not pretty enough, too damaged, too smart".

1._____

2._____

3._____

4._____

5._____

6._____

7._____

8._____

9._____

10._____

Limiting beliefs are the ultimate bliss killers. Use this space to take back your power by creating personal power mantras for yourself. Choose your new beliefs and say them everyday!

The strongest action for a woman is to **LOVE** herself, **BE** herself, and **SHINE** amongst those who never believed *she* could.

FORGIVENESS

LETTING IT ALL GO

I was always told that if we experience any resistance in our lives, its probably tied to forgiveness. However, forgiveness isn't always about forgiving someone else, it is most often times forgiveness for ourselves that we truly need in order to flourish.

For me, this was a hard concept to grasp, after all why would I need to forgive myself for what someone else did *to me*? It wasn't until I went to a seminar about success that painted the picture very clearly. I was led to investigate my entrepreneurial history for certain things like procrastination, failure, doubt, indecision, etc. These are they types of things we do without any acknowledgement, so these memories stay stuck in our subconscious minds just awaiting for them to come up again. These limiting traits now feel comfortable to us, so we will repeat them over and over because it has become the natural thing for us to do.

The only way out is through forgiveness.

When we begin to take responsibility for our lives and the circumstances that play out, we can begin to evolve and heal. We must acknowledge these times that we have betrayed or abandoned ourselves by actions that didn't serve us in our life, then forgive the action and move on.

It's a bit like decluttering work, except in this case we are decluttering our subconscious mind and heart. An easy way to do this is by using the Ho'oponopono Prayer we learned earlier in the book...

I LOVE YOU

I'M SORRY

PLEASE FORGIVE ME

THANK YOU

Saying this and really meaning it, will clear up anything that needs to be forgiven in your mind, body and soul.

I really want us to work on forgiving ourselves for anything that we allowed ourselves to go through, anything we bought that we shouldn't have, anything we didn't eat that we wanted to or anything we said yes to when we wanted to say no. This is referred to as shadow work and clearing out the cobwebs of our souls. We are the ones who are responsible for our lives and taking on that responsibility will serve as a massive catalyst for change and allow your inner self to really shine. Let's take some time to dig a little deeper into this work.

What do I need to forgive myself for? In what ways have I abounded myself or let myself down?

1._____

2._____

3._____

4._____

5._____

6._____

7._____

8._____

9._____

10._____

11._____

12._____

13._____

What did I do or did not do that I need to acknowledge and let go of. . .

1. _____

2. _____

3. _____

4. _____

5. _____

6. _____

7. _____

8. _____

9. _____

10. _____

11. _____

12. _____

13. _____

Trust the wait.
Embrace the
uncertainty.
Enjoy the beauty of
becoming.
When nothing is certain,
anything is
possible.

ILLUMINATION

POWERFUL MANIFESTATION

This is my favorite part of this journal. Mostly because at this point you have most likely chipped away at your hard clay exterior and are beginning to see your golden essence shine through. It's your time for illumination, your time to shine!

You are magical, radiant, beautiful, soulful, wonderful, awe inspiring and majorly powerful! It's time for you to step into your power. Now that you are operating from a bliss vibes only, no matter what mindset, you are aligned with the life of your dreams.

I am going to share with you my personal process for getting in that manifesting alignment so you will naturally draw to you more things that make you feel blissful. Don't let your mind trick you into thinking that its more difficult than it actually is. It's meant to be easy, you just have to believe it in order to receive it.

An amazing thing happens when you surround yourself with **blissful**, positive, appreciative, love filled people…

Your life fills with **bliss**, positivity, appreciation and love.

8 STEPS TO MANIFESTING YOUR DREAMS

1. Get clear on what it is that you really want your life to look like.

2. Let go of anything that doesn't align with your vision. This is where you make Bliss Vibes Only a non-negotiable barometer for everything in your life.

3. Get super grateful for the things that you currently have and are experiencing. Feel the emotion of joy.

4. Visualize yourself at your best, highest, most amazing version of you and begin to bring that energy out into your daily life.

5. Believe that what you desire is meant for you.

6. Write, say and repeat affirmations that align with your dream life.

7. Surround yourself with things that make you blissfully happy. This is so important when it comes to your home, car and office. You must love all the things that surround you.

8. Surrender and Allow. Step into your divine feminine queen, best version of yourself who is ready to actually allow her dreams to come into her life without resistance.

WHAT I WANT TO MANIFEST...

1. $400k/year income
2. $6600 right now for electrology school
3. A beautiful home in Texas with a 2 bedroom ADU & pool & shop
4. A successful electrology business
5. A successful children's boutique/consignment store
6. A wellness/yoga retreat with husband
7. lifelong friendships
8. A fulltime caregiver for Cavan
9. weekly date nights with husband
10.
11.
12.

WHAT I WANT TO EXPERIENCE IN MY LIFE...

1. Traveling to Paris, Greece, Ireland, Egypt, Japan +
2. Having grandkids
3.
4.
5.
6.
7.
8.
9.
10.
11.
12.

THINGS I NEED TO LET GO OF...

1. _____

2. _____

3. _____

4. _____

5. _____

6. _____

7. _____

8. _____

9. _____

10. _____

11. _____

12. _____

PEOPLE I NEED TO LET GO OF...

1. _____

2. _____

3. _____

4. _____

5. _____

6. _____

7. _____

8. _____

9. _____

10. _____

11. _____

12. _____

THINGS I AM GRATEFUL FOR...

1._____

2._____

3._____

4._____

5._____

6._____

7._____

8._____

9._____

10._____

11._____

12._____

THINGS I AM GRATEFUL FOR...

1. _____

2. _____

3. _____

4. _____

5. _____

6. _____

7. _____

8. _____

9. _____

10. _____

11. _____

12. _____

QUALITIES OF MY HIGEST SELF...

1._____

2._____

3._____

4._____

5._____

6._____

7._____

8._____

9._____

10._____

11._____

12._____

THINGS MY HIGHEST SELF LOVES TO DO...

1. _____

2. _____

3. _____

4. _____

5. _____

6. _____

7. _____

8. _____

9. _____

10. _____

11. _____

12. _____

AFFIRMATIONS THAT I LOVE...

1._____

2._____

3._____

4._____

5._____

6._____

7._____

8._____

9._____

10._____

11._____

12._____

I AM WORTHY OF...

1. _____

2. _____

3. _____

4. _____

5. _____

6. _____

7. _____

8. _____

9. _____

10. _____

11. _____

12. _____

Focus on the **powerful**, euphoric, **magical**, synchronistic, **beautiful** parts of life, and the **universe** will keep giving them to you.

DIVINE FEMININE

It won't take long before you begin to experience magical moments in your life. When you are in alignment, feeling the flow and plugged into your divine feminine you are now set up to be in a constant state of receiving all the things of bliss.

Nothing is a random coincidence, everything happens in perfect divine order. Think of yourself as a queen, so connected to her divine feminine that you have no choice but to receive all the beautiful things that are meant for you. Be sure to acknowledge and appreciate the synchronicities that begin to appear out of nowhere.

You want to make sure to keep a log of all these beautiful synchronicities that happen for you, so more of them keep coming. Things like someone you just thought of calls you out of the blue, you receive an unexpected check in the mail, someone buys your coffee, you keep seeing repeating angel numbers, you are in the right place at the right time, etc.

DIVINE, BLISSFUL & MAGICAL MOMENTS...

DATE: _____

_____
_____
_____
_____
_____
_____
_____
_____
_____
_____
_____
_____

DATE: _____

_____
_____
_____
_____
_____
_____
_____
_____
_____
_____
_____
_____

DIVINE, BLISSFUL & MAGICAL MOMENTS...

DATE: _____

_____
_____
_____
_____
_____
_____
_____
_____
_____
_____
_____

DATE: _____

_____
_____
_____
_____
_____
_____
_____
_____
_____
_____
_____
_____
_____

DIVINE, BLISSFUL & MAGICAL MOMENTS...

DATE: _____

_____
_____
_____
_____
_____
_____
_____
_____
_____
_____
_____
_____

DATE: _____

_____
_____
_____
_____
_____
_____
_____
_____
_____
_____
_____
_____
_____

"Your sacred space is where you can find yourself over and over again."
-Joseph Campbell

Made in the USA
Las Vegas, NV
10 March 2022